Human Ti

Duncan Forbes

Human Time

First published in 2020
by Voicemail Press
9 High Street
Prestbury
Cheltenham GL52 3AR

ISBN 978-1-9163680-0-2

A CIP record for this title is available from the British Library

Designed in Bembo by Servis Filmsetting
and printed in Wales by Gomer Press

CONTENTS

By Air

Astonishing to think
That not so long ago
First the Brothers Wright
Then Louis Blériot
Initiated flight.

And strapped into a seat
Now we can choose a drink,
Tomato juice, red wine,
Some music or a film
At 30,000 feet.

Remarkable to know
That aviation fuel,
Once vegetable remains,
Comes from the earth as oil
And energises planes.

Comforting to presume
The cabin's pressurised
And instruments of flight
Are skilfully devised
To navigate the night.

Consoling to believe
The forces that can heave
The weight of this machine
Above the ocean waves
And alpine mountain scene.

Strange to be conscious of
The distant sea below
And absent sky above
Where cloud formations flow
Detached from all we love.

A MOMENT

There it is, the wren.
Keep still. Breathe in.
The tiny bird
with stumpy tail
has landed near
the windowsill
and moves from twig to stem
as quietly as rain.

Feathered and breathing,
it matches its portrait
on the bronze farthings
of my childhood
sixty years ago
but look away
and it has gone again
from then to now.

There in the corner of a darkened field,
Deer in a group were eating midnight corn,
A family of grazing fallow deer
With dappled does and here and there a fawn
Outside the planted area of the square,
Their heads illuminated in our headlights where
We were returning from the theatre late
(Some tragic tanglement of human kind)
And watched the deer herd as they stood and ate
The ears of ripened corn from tawny stalks,
The legs of deer and hollow stems of grain,
Bowed heads of fallow deer on supple necks,
A harvest festival of night and gold,
The scene lit up by other lives revealed.

CELLAR DWELLER

What is that spider called
that lives on cellar walls and floors
and looks like a ball of hair
with mind and legs of its own?

Walking on filament stilts,
it weaves its minimal webs
though what can it catch at all
but a skeletal ghost of a meal?

And yet it breathes and breeds,
a dingy dungeon wisp
in flaking paintwork and dust
where woodlice curl to a crisp.

The cosmos is so vast
and particles so small
I think I'm glad to be
for all our crimes and grime
a human after all
now at this present time
which soon will be the past.

Here on this biosphere,
the molecules we breathe
and H_2O we drink
are held by gravity
in forces which cohere
the whole atomic seethe
or so we like to think.

I simplify of course.
I'm not a physicist
who thinks in terms of force
or energy and mass
and I am somewhat loath
to see what may exist
as wave and particle both.

'What then is quantum time
and what is quantum space?'
Why are you asking me,
I who believe in days
and measure space where I'm
existing in the flesh
with human body and face?

The microscopic mind
in macrocosmic space
tries to invent or find
some unifying phrase
until enquiry yields
the theory of the day,
co-variant quantum fields.

Although our heads contain
neurons and synapses
rather than megabytes,
I do not have the brain,
the aptitudes and traits
to grasp or entertain
such complex postulates.

I'm glad I'm not a quark
with a nano-second life
or a galaxy miles across,
light-years from spark to dark;
I prefer consciousness,
perplexed by love and loss
and all we have to guess.

The school of dolphins. Remember them?
They surface in the mind again mid-ocean
and reaffirm themselves as fellow mammals.
Golfinhos! said to be common dolphins
but not to us who marvel at their being.

We watch the shapes distorted underwater,
the dark triangular shadow of the dorsal fin,
sparkle of sunlight on their steel-grey flanks,
the brisk propulsive tail-fins and finesse,
as dolphins glide and glisten round the boat.

We admire the muscle missiles of torpedo bodies
splashing the semi-precious drops of whitened water
shining in sunlight for the moving moment.
We share the close-up views of calf and cow,
eyes open, blowholes breathing.

We cannot count how many dolphins now
are swimming here. Playing as water plays,
they ply the supple waves
and weave their underwater wanderings
and so we try to comprehend

their alien dialects of clicks and squeaks,
the briny taste of fish on tooth and tongue,
the sights of sunlight searching underwater,
the submarine smells and echoes,
forests of kelp and oceanographies.

And then they dive, swimming away from air and sky
into those darkened depths of their marine world,
while we are here marooned in ours
which is not ours and never was,
as dolphins disappear below our wake.

What would you say, what would you do
If you could see us sitting now
Assembled here because of you
And all you meant to each of us?

What music would you want to hear,
What formula of words approve
Or have you left the choice to us
Not to be sanctimonious?

What send-off or what eulogy,
What sort of ceremonial
Could lend a kind of harmony
To what lies underneath it all?

You shared in life's vicissitudes,
Its temperamental downs and ups,
Its solace and beatitudes,
Raising of glasses and dashed hopes.

We offer thanks and afterwards,
With all we cannot know or guess,
We speak of you, exchanging words
Which are inadequate to express

Your life-enhancing liveliness,
The works of art and meals once shared,
The kindnesses until the news
Of your decline and dying spread.

The future's what we can't foresee,
The past cannot be repossessed
But now and in the meantime we
Remember you and at your best.

DISUSED DRINKING FOUNTAIN

The public are expected to protect
From injury that which is erected
For the public good. And now it is protected,
This Grade II-listed disused drinking fountain
In Charlton Kings. There on its westward face
Is carved a bas-relief of Jesus with
The woman at the well (John Chapter 4).
As in Samaria, so in Cheltenham
Before clean running water blessed each home.
Dilapidated, vandalised, polluted,
Ignored by time and traffic, now restored.
Above the dry, pink granite drinking bow,
These seven words, carved capitals in stone,
Proclaim: PRAISE GOD FROM WHOM ALL BLESSINGS FLOW.

So here again we find this wayside shrine
Under its spire, a consecrated fountain,
Where living water used to flow and shine
To quench the thirst of wayfarers and horses,
Assuaging dry throats and refreshing faces.
In grinding glacier and in cloud formation,
It thawed, evaporated, sparkled, froze
From mountain range and dewdrop to the ocean.
Under the skies each season, water flows
To bring life to this planet whose ablution
Remains as liquid as our ancestry;
Born to its waters, later when we die
It is one solvent in our mystery
And shall be till its influence runs dry.

DOZENS

Six am and dark in December.
A lorry pulls into the farmyard
and the driver lowers a ramp with a crash.

We enter the stench of the henhouse,
a low hangar as long as a runway
with thousands of fowls in pungent cacophony.

Janet collects the dung-smeared eggs,
smooth dumb miracles of replication,
and carries them to the cleaner.

Our job is to empty the noisy cages,
to reach through each trapdoor of wire
and garner the chickens in handfuls of six.

Some of them shit themselves in panic.
Some flutter desperately biting at gloves.
Some are pecked naked already and thin.

Others lie dead, their carcases darkened
and smelly, eyes white as the pips
in an unripe Discovery apple.

Our left hand tendons aching
round six bony legs and feet,
we walk with each bundle of feathers and heads

hanging between the rows of prisoners
into the cleansed silence of starlight
to the twin doors of the transportation cages.

When dawn eventually breaks over the hills,
the sun is yellow as egg yolk, the clouds
streaky like bacon and the lorry says Shippams.

Next day, we remove the cockerels
from the fresh batches, wring their rainbow necks
and throw their twitching corpses to the pigs.

Underneath an angel,
the risen Christ appears,
a halo round his head.
Left hand on the handle,
he's leaning on a spade,
right hand raised in blessing,
neat wounds in hands and feet
and, wrapped in glowing grave clothes
backlit by April sunlight,
he stands there in the garden.

In the other window,
Mary Magdalene,
anxious and distressed,
thought he was the gardener
and wondered where they'd placed
the corpse from the empty tomb
but now she kneels dismayed
to recognise 'Rabboni'
in the transfigured person
the risen Christ, her lord.

I am the resurrection,
says Jesus, and the life,
which raises the objections
of doubt and unbelief.
Under the skies of Lincolnshire
beyond the tended graves,
only the sunlight resurrects
the landscape into leaf.
Meanwhile the River Witham
winds seaward to the sea.

Is it a ghost in the machine,
This silver surfer on the screen?
No, it's me and I look green
Reflected in the plastic top
Here on a laptop on my lap
And now I'm listening to a rap
By Eminem, a pseudonym
For Marshal Mathers III, yes him,
A man from the Chicago scene
Who's talking big and acting mean
On top of a building storeys high,
A suicidal Superman
About to fall, about to fly
But who knows where and who cares why,
Chicago, Michigan, Detroit,
Into some cyberspace or void.
He's standing on the brink and talking
From a skyscraper top and walking
Ready to fly like Peter Pan
But brooding like a wounded man
With drumbeat and a backing choir
On loneliness despair desire,
A stream of consciousness no less
Where life's an existential mess,
A fast and furious word assault,
A four-minute rant of finding fault,
And here I am with Eminem
I'm watching him while he's with them,
From gilded youth to grumpy age
From stroppy young to senior rage
Now all the world's a bloody stage,
The globe's a ball and stars a cage

Until you die and turn the page
Then nothing's left to read or ride
While cells commit their suicide
And atoms humble human pride.

FOSSIL RECORD

I should like to become a fossil;
it would be a singular honour
and posthumous decoration.
My dying wish is not to be made ash
by the gas fires of a crematorium
but lay my naked corpse in shallow water
with sediment, silt or mud.
Let the soft tissues dissolve
or be eaten by hungry creatures
until the bare skeleton
can lie under the weight
of a rock formation
and let the processes
of petrifaction begin.
Teeth and bone are replaced by chemicals
much more slowly than the speed
at which a fingernail once grew.
Jawbone. Humerus. Ribcage. Skull.
Till I is an anonymous
monument of stone,
a specimen from the Anthropocene,
a hominid known or unknown
by whatever noun is then in fashion
or by none and no one.

GRAFFITI

A would-be graffiti artist
who dislikes vandalism,
I read on a white Thames Water van
the words *Together let's beat the drought
Ask driver for details*
and I want to Tippex out
the d of driver.

Likewise at Reading Station
I should like to add some letters
to the lit-up signs
so they announce the town's arrival
as DREADING READING SPREADING
all the way down the platform
DREADING READING SPREADING
from London to Penzance.

It's down a private lane with potholed dips
And passing places. There are infrequent signs
To help you in the dubious wayward search
For why you think you might have come so far
And for St Michael and All Angels Church.

Open the large closed door which might be locked
And you go back to Venice now and here.
Nothing prepares you for the pristine shock
Of white and gold inside this village church
In Worcestershire. Italianate baroque!

The stained glass windows are not just stained glass
But glass enamelling which floods each pane
With painted colours for New Testament scenes
Except the Golden Calf. Sleter's designs
Were realised by Joshua Price and Sons.

And there it stands: the Foley monument carved
By J.M. Rysbrach in Carrara marble,
The tallest and best industrial wealth could own,
A huge unwieldy shrine to family dead,
With lifesize figures in unlifelike stone.

The ceiling images are astonishing;
Antonio Bellucci painted them:
A grand Ascension into heaven above,
Flanked by Nativity and Lamentation,
Takes Christ in majesty to God of Love.

The paintings and the church have been restored
To former glories by conservators' arts,
As if we, by retouching, could renew
The healing passion and the creed of faith
If only they seemed credible or true.

But here's a mausoleum of beliefs,
A painted sepulchre of white and gold
Whose splendid iconographies pretend
That time is an immortal like a god
And deaths are a beginning not an end.

Grounded and close-to,
they look like clockwork toys
wearing oily jackets
of rainbow-flecked feathers,
walking jerkily on stiff pink legs.
Their song is torn tin,
metal on metal squealing

But their evening event at the end of the day
    is a practical fractal enacted,
an aerial ballet of ecstatic display.
Their elliptical shape has a loop and a leap
    where hundreds of starlings, thousands of birds,
        take to the sky in a scatter of letters or swerve of a curve.

Oh how we admire and long to capture
    the indelible ephemeral memory
of these murmurations of starlings,
a river of birds, imploding, exploding,
though not long ago in their fertilized eggs,
    now a flexible flock in sinuous flux,
        a consensus condensing
            which then consents to cohere
                and go here hither hence.

Their patterns confuse and elude,
    the instinctual interlinking of each bird,
their wonderful weavings of wingbeats on silence
    before roosting and resting in safety of numbers,
        a swirling, wheeling mass of starling
            and starlings whirring and flying as one
                though conscious of seven,

like particles in a quantum field
    where the field is the sky and the sky endless
       and whether or not we believe,
   you or I, in a heaven or ever
here's an empirical miracle
  of lyrical flight and feather.

Retired persons are not necessarily
retiring or withdrawn
although we are entitled to feel tired
and/or rejuvenated
by our superannuated state.

In France they are *en retraite*
or they have retreated.
In Italy they are *pensionati*
if they are lucky
and in Germany *Rentner.*
In Spain they are *jubilados*
and in Portugal simply
reformados.

Happy euphemisms!
In the fullness of time
as a senior senior citizen
you will have to re-retire
stateless into a non-state where
not one word of language
exists in the breathless air.

Heartener and Hearer

I met you twice, once old, once young,
And in the government of the tongue
There shone intelligence and grace,
Eyes lighting up your thoughtful face,

Exponent of the maker's craft
By which a word is curved or carved
Into a shape by gift or graft
And lives its life beyond the grave.

When Eliot and Auden died
We looked for one who purified
The troubled dialect of the tribe
To be its consecrated scribe

And you were he, our mind and mentor,
Scholar, poet and inventor;
This man of letters understood
The shattered bones of shedding blood.

Your scrutiny looked deep and hard
At selves beyond all self-regard
And in each shrewd analysis
You saw what should be and what is.

They called your language Heaneyese,
Earthy and grounded, but like trees
It could soar skyward from its roots
Bearing exotic and strange fruits.

Religion: catholic in the sense
You wondered whither, why and whence,
At little miracles of loaves
And fishes in our humble lives.

'Bog-eyed Narcissus', so you joked
But we knew then the fun you poked
At your expense only endeared
A venerator now revered.

'Irish poets, learn your trade,
Sing whatever is well-made'
And so you did with lyric grace
To reappraise the human race.

Alert, concerned, with tact that warmed,
Dear Seamus Heaney, you confirmed
That life's a blessing and to bless
We need love's universal yes.

Let us take heart from your example,
Never extreme or over-simple;
Poet, exemplar, show us ways
To tell the truth and yet to praise.

HIPPOCAMPUS

Look for the tail's prehensile curl
around the seagrass or the coral.
What have we here in the shape of an S?
A curvilinear upright fish
made for disguise and camouflage
swaying like seaweed in the tide,
a chess-piece knight with dragonish tail.

Head of a horse no horse has seen,
each wears a different coronet.
Its eyes like a chameleon's
move independently for food
which burrows, clings to plants or floats.
Through a long snout of bony plates,
it sucks minute crustaceans in.

The private lives of either sex
intrigue marine biologists.
They bond for life and value touch.
The female wanders while the male
is pregnant with the fertile eggs,
expelling from his ventral pouch
fry to face currents and the tides.

Prime predators aren't crabs or gulls
but human hands with nets and trawls,
the fishermen who sell them on,
inedible exoskeletons,
sundried to the medicine trade.
Bones ground to dust, they only breed
to cure the credulous of disease.

We like to watch seahorses swim,
fins behind eyes and dorsal fin
fanning the water in slow motion,
curios in an aquarium
or emblem of the planet Ocean
misnamed Earth by our admission
as dying for life and oxygen.

HOME

I haven't found a town
That I can call my own,
I haven't found a place
Where I can head for home,
Nor have I seen the face
That I cannot disown
As just a passing phase
On transitory ground;
An exit from the maze
Has also to be found.

I haven't made the time
To make my feelings known
But you're the only one
In whom I find my own
Affinity and base,
Identity and home;
You are the place where I'm
Most likely to be found
And all I've ever known
Of certitude and grace.

IN OTHER WORDS

Our tenuous tenancy today
Has been and gone tomorrow.
The future comes but come what may
No time is ours to borrow.
The afterlives of yesterday
Are synonyms for sorrow.

By which I mean it's not my way –
I know it's sentimental –
But even so I want to say
While time extends its rental
That I have valued every day
When you've been kind and gentle.

In other words I love you now
I cannot tell you why or how
But take it as a lover's vow,
Not miserly nor mental,
But fully meant and meaning all.

IN THE CHURCHYARD

On a Saturday afternoon,
a courting couple lay
on the grass between two graves.
Courting was once the word
for the intertwining of youth
in what are now olden days
though peopled nevertheless
in the same time-honoured ways.

A woman walking a dog
looked on and disapproved
of inconsiderate young.
The dog thought – who knows what? –
but when she walked he moved
being on a leather lead
and followed her at a trot
away from the makings of love.

Gravestones, names and dates
are all that is left of those
who have populated the place
with so many senior dead
where bones adjust to the tomb
and ashes are scattered above
with no memories of their time,
intensities or love.

In the Wardrobe

If soon I do not wear
all of the clothes I've bought,
some will be unworn still
by the time I shuffle off
and leave them in my will.

Yes, there's a leather jacket
and a second-hand cowboy hat
from Prescott Arizona
in which I look a prat
but it's time to wear them out.

I must don the brightest colours
and then select such clothes
as suit my shape and size
before I die and doff
all costume and disguise.

All of those empty clothes
in pink, red, blue and green
like purple moleskin trousers
are hanging on a rail,
unused and still unseen.

It is time to show them off
before I'm too decrepit
either to care or choose
the colour and cut of cloth
or a pair of snazzy shoes.

Forever young like Peter Pan,
That hitherto has been the plan
But whinge and twinge turn to disease
Like osteo-arthritic knees.
I've got two now and number one
Has had an operation done,
Till rheumatoid arthritis hits
And chews the aging joints to bits.

And next when cancer wants you dead
There's chemotherapy to dread
With radiation of the growth
Which feels like death and dying both,
Concomitant with loss of hair,
Fresh miseries and dark despair,
Cadaverous loss of appetite
And bleaker wakings in the night.

Which way to go and how is best?
Not stroke nor cardiac arrest.
I've seen two victims of a stroke,
Survivors when the engine broke,
And knew them both before and after.
Before, normality and laughter:
Now disabilities for life,
A wheel-chair and a carer-wife.

Dementia, yes, I've seen that too
And know what the disease can do
To disconnect you and I'd rather
Not suffer from it like my father,
Otherwise healthy in physique,
But growing more senile every week
Until he lost all speech and fell
Leaving him paralysed as well.

Phlegethon, Acheron, Lethe, Styx:
The afterlives to me mean nix
For in my credo I confess
That death means loss of consciousness,
Decomposition and decay,
Not resurrection's Judgement Day.
My dying wish if I survive
Is not to be buried while alive.

I need a drink which I define
As two plus units of red wine
And yet I fear the glum prognosis
For this my liver of cirrhosis.
Advance with care. Proceed with caution.
You have to see things in proportion
But need more than a sense of humour
To cope with a malignant tumour.

I'm scared of dying and of pain –
I'd rather morphine in the brain
Though what in essence is that fear
But of not knowing why we're here?
Threescore years plus ten or twenty
Do for most and feel like plenty
But as the end draws ever nearer
The days and living both seem dearer.

So do most people whom we knew
As all the truisms come true
And it's when push comes back to shove
About this leaving all we love
And recognising far too late
Because mortality's our fate
That what life was is wonderful
From start to end, once and for all.

Redbacked and mature,
landlocked sockeye salmon
with haunted skull-like faces
set their green heads
against the current,
intent on mating
and laying their eggs
in the gravel for males
to fertilize with milt.

Shoals of kokanee
were swimming upstream
to spawn and die,
flipping and flapping
their way over dams
in the spawning channels.

Mallards were diving
to guzzle the eggs.
Ravens and herring-gulls
swooped on the bodies.
High above on a pine-tree,
an osprey was watching
life in its cycle,
fish in their folly,
food in its chain.

MAKE AND MEND

I remember the wooden clothes horse,
the ironing board and pungent hiss of steam
when stainlessly hot steel met moistened cloth.
The wooden darning egg in the sewing-basket
made from a fabric-covered cardboard box.
The booklet of cloth, each leaf containing needles
of different sizes and the box of pins
and safety-pins. The tin of buttons.
The wooden reels of many-coloured threads,
sewing-machine and its excited bobbin,
the pinking-shears with their serrated edges.
The concentration on your motherly face
as first you licked the cotton straight and then
threaded the filament through the needle's eye.
I can imagine you at work tonight
under the lamp-light of an Anglepoise,
that frown of concentration on your face,
sewing or darning to the radio
and yet it's over sixty years ago
and I have only memories of you now,
till love that turns to loss is love again.

MISSING UNCLES

In a sepia photograph
I see great uncle Stephen Vine,
a strangely adolescent man,
dressed in khaki for the grave.

Brother of Winifred (née Vine)
to whom she gave a sister's love
never returned from that last leave
hoping he would not die in vain.

Uncle Sandy paid the price
for enlisting under age
by fighting for the privilege
of combat with the Japanese.

Men who gave their lives for what?
Kings George V and George VI
in past imperial politics?
War, just war and then goodnight

leaving our only uncle Tom
who can't be drawn on what he did
or what he thought when Sandy died.
It must have been a cruel time.

At least my father's line survived
Sandy Wilson, Stephen Vine,
those uncles dead before their prime,
or else I'd not be here alive.

MOONLIGHT

Moonrise over the sea.
Sunset over the land.
Exquisite is the word
after a cloudless day
for the wonders of the world.
Planet and moon rotate,
satellite mirrors the sun,
waves reflect the light
and the moon like a faceless clock
illuminates the scene
and clarifies the mind,
unique but not alone
as day turns into night
and years to eras fade.

Exquisite is the word
as you and I agree
or would do if we were
together when we heard
water cleanse the sand
or land resist the sea
with cliffs of crumbling rock
under a sunlit moon,
though I feel part resigned
that we may never see
together from where you stand
unique but not alone
sunset over the land,
moonrise over the sea.

Where are all the femmes fatales
Who were once foetal in the womb
Whose images persist on film?
What is the afterlife to them?
What do they look like in the mirror
Now that night has closed their era?
What good was clothing or allure,
Perfumed languor, suntanned vigour
Or sands of time to hour-glass figure?

Brigitte Bardot tends to dogs.
World-famous Greta Garbo chose
To shun her fame as a recluse.
Where's Claudia Cardinale now
Or Gina Lollobrigida
And Marilyn (Norma Jean) Monroe
('A suicide kills two, you know')
While Ursula Andress on a beach
Enacts a modern birth of Venus?

Then there's Rock Hudson and Clark Gable,
Brando in his *Streetcar* prime
Before the bloated mumbler came,
Gregory Peck and Cary Grant,
James Dean, Steve McQueen and Elvis
And all the other men who aren't,
Paul Newman, Mitchum and John Wayne –
You can supply the names yourselves:
We are all acting out our lives.

The moving image is a still
Illusion on a lighted screen:
Time a dimension we are in
From birth to death and what they mean.
Where have they gone, the days and years?
Gone like Mesozoic snow,
Gone like Babylon and Troy,
Miles away and long ago
Till everybody disappears.

I've given up the ghost
and kicked the bucket.
I've snuffed it. Am deceased
and not just past it
but passed on and forever
or as they now say passed
as if it's an exam,
this being not. Not being am.
Are you aghast? I'm not.
I've passed away. I've gone.
Helped by cremation
and the undertaker,
I'm pushing up the daisies
and gone to meet my maker
who may be absent too
or else I've gone to blazes,
depends on point of view,
the way of all dead flesh.
It's over in a flash.
The ticker tocks and then
it's cardiac arrest.
You have no breath, no zest.
It's over, out, paroled.
Stock-still. Stone-dead. Stone-cold.
No more. I've turned the page
and reached the end of age.
My deathday's now a date
and yes I am the late ...

NEVERENDUM

You find a complex question
and you simplify it so.
You call a referendum
and you make it YES or NO.
You think of an addendum
and you call it IN or OUT.
You disunite the kingdom
and you think it's worth a shout.
You hector the electorate,
you posture, lie, deceive,
till many in the plebiscite
can doubt what you believe.
Then you ask them in a ballot
to vote REMAIN or LEAVE
and you're left with one agendum
and with grievances to grieve.

New Eyes Each Year

(Hull University 2017)

In the City of Culture
There's an exhibition where,
Suspended by grey braces,
A beige, capacious pair
Of Philip Larkin's trousers
Is hanging in the air,
As if the Larkin essence
Were trouserless despair.

They match his gutted diaries
With only covers left
And on display in cases,
Without the poet's deft
Descriptions of his daily
Warp and woe and weft,
Fed to the library shredder
And of his words bereft.

NUTHATCH

I wait and catch
a glimpse of her
or him: the nuthatch
(*sitta europaea*)
alighting on the perch
to feed on treats
and taste the insides
of sunflower seeds.

Eye-stripe. Black beak.
Woodpecker's head
on agile legs
with steel-blue plumage
over buff-orange belly,
it was not long ago
in a clutch of white eggs
freckled with red.

And it has taken me
all these years
to acknowledge how
the sight of a bird
can be revered
in the here and now
as I watch it and
the nuthatch come and go.

In Aljezur we took a walk
And paused above the river where,
Among the rushes, swifts and fish,
We saw a water-snake drink the air
Before the reptile rippled back
And watched until an azure flash
Flew from the bridge to walnut tree,
A kingfisher in sudden flight,
A memorised epiphany
Almost before it came and went,
Electric blue and heaven-sent,
To fish and feed downriver where
The sailing vessels once had moved
Beside the town of Aljezur.

And then we climbed the cobbled hill
Past bees and flowers in summer heat
And entered by the castle gate
To read about the ancient site:
A Moorish cistern now caught rain
Where silos once had stored the grain.
We heard the cowbells on the wind
And then imagined in the sound
The medieval settlement.
On water-meadows down below
Across the rich alluvial plain,
Neat vegetables in row on row,
Potatoes, onions, maize and beans,
In miniature abundance grow.

Where codes and cultures rose and fell,
We saw a fragile butterfly
Land on a flower long-since dry
And imitate its petals when
It opened up white marbled wings.
We watched a stork rise high above
The plain, the hill, the citadel,
In aerial serenity
As if it were a symbol of
The continuities of life
When all its blessings feel like love:
We saw a kingfisher for sure
And watched a stork on thermals soar
One afternoon in Aljezur.

Sometimes today seems narrow
until at last we go
to the infinite tomorrow
which we shall never know

unless the falser promises
prove unbelief untrue
and we can leave the premises
inhuman but anew.

OXFORD PARKWAY

I catch the train from busy Marylebone
to Oxford Parkway and when I alight
pulling my case on wheels
I see the crowded car park, and I think
so many machines. So many
locked rooms on wheels,
engines, metal, oil and fossil fuels.

Then I notice a creature zigzag lolloping
along the tarmac between two rows
of parked cars. A small dog with long ears?
'Good heavens,' I say aloud to myself,
'It's a hare.' A hare
in the slant October sunlight
and I wish it (by which I mean him or her)
I wish that hare in fields and grass elsewhere
under the sunlight or the distant stars.

PALE SUNLIGHT ON BLACK HILL

In memory of David Prentice
(1936–2014)

Islands of land inland, the inselbergs
Emerge above the midland plain,
A mountain range in miniature.
England lies east, Wales to the west.
Underneath Worcester Beacon is the solid ground
Which flowed as molten rock
In Cambrian or Pre-Cambrian times.
Look up. Look back.

Beside this creased and undulating crest,
Iron Age inhabitants guard British Camp.
Drovers tread the old salt route from Droitwich.
Adders and dormice here survive
In bracken, under brambles.
Auden is meeting Erika Mann at Malvern Wells.
Tolkien and Lewis imagine a middle earth
Where hikers and bikers now erode conservators' turf.
A teashop tempts with bacon sandwiches.
In sunlight rainclouds chase their shadows
From pasturelands across the water meadows.
Flying above, a buzzard and a lark
Inspire an Edward Elgar and his music.
And in a medieval manuscript
On a May morning on the Malverne Hills
A ploughman called Piers dreams
But not of the Victorian spa with posh hotels
Nor of the Darwins' daughter and her little grave.

Though death's a given, David, life's a gift.
With your reed pen and active mind
You observed this spine and spirit of the Malverns
In painting after painting, year on year,
Season by season and in all the weathers,
Each numinous picture a complete quotation,
Its title like a poem. Your paintings celebrate
The land and skyscape's ever-changing palette,
While each new day alive reminds us of
The star we see as light and feel as warmth,
The free and open air we breathe for now,
Our fragile tenancies of all we know.

Encircled in a goldfish pond,
The triple orbits were aligned,
The sun, the moon and earth beyond,
As if each moment is designed.

The mirror was the water's round
On which the sun's reflection played
And travelling without a sound
The moon turned sunlight into shade.

I watched it in a bucket once,
The sunlight sixty years ago
Reduced to insignificance
As if it lost its fiery glow.

At more than twice the speed of sound
The silent moon eclipsed the sun.
Its shadow moved across the ground
And cosmic geometries were one.

And here again it's happened now.
A visible eclipse appears
And each return reminds us how
We measure earthly months and years.

Today's the day, I say.
No need to hesitate.
Don't dawdle on the way,
Prevaricate or wait.

But then a thing like doubt
Begins to change the route,
Foreseeing no way out
Which hindsight can't dispute.

The self itself begins
To wonder what it is.
No answers. Many signs.
More questions than a quiz.

And looking at the leap,
What is it that prevents
A dreamer counting sheep
From sliding off the fence?

What dilatory lapse
Infects the motive will
With maybe and perhaps,
Unless, if or until?

Instead of facing facts
I ponder and then pause
To quantify effects
And contemplate the cause.

What have I done today
But feed the appetite,
Procrastinate, delay
And fraternise with night?

What shall we do tomorrow
But criticise today
On time we start to borrow
From yesterday's delay?

So there they are in black and white,
The Oxford crew of '38.
By now I know their surnames too
And I can name them stern to bow.
They're facing backwards as they race
Towards the future's unknown prize.

And there he is again, dark-haired,
Taking in air and breathing hard,
My father pulling on an oar,
A well-developed number 4
Who does not know me for his son,
The war yet to be fought and won.

And of that crew, three men at least,
Young, Cherry, Merifield, were lost,
Two in the Mediterranean zone,
Then Squadron-Leader Dinghy Young
Who could not once more paddle home
Across the North Sea's darkened foam.

Here by a photographic plate
The spray is stopped in air as light,
The moment captured, time a frame,
And somewhere on the tidal Thames
The Oxford oars of '38
Are giving all and all too late.

I wake and find it bleak week after week.
I fake a friendly face to take my place.
I fold the social whirl into a world
And hope that no escape will give me scope.
I think therefore I drink to drown and sink.
Desires are a disease of mortal needs.
I act and then dissect the foregone fact.
I fail and then defile my failure's fault.
The past is memory lost which can't be faced,
The present an incessant is and isn't,
The future is anew without a feature.
I wish for what the flesh cannot express.
I need your help to guide me to be freed
And make from my mistakes a new mystique.
I crave your lasting love to be and thrive.
I grieve for all alive that I must leave.
I long to right the wrong and to belong.
For once give me a chance, a chance to change.
Convince my doubts' defence to doubt their sense.
Divide me from my pride which I evade
And bless my thoughts with yes and nonetheless.
Amen is what I mean and what you meant.
Not night. Not infinite. Not now. Not yet.

QUIET NEIGHBOURS

A candelabrum in the month of May,
The chestnut tree is fighting a disease.
The gravestones act as sundials all day long
While shadows shift from westward round to east,
Prostrate upon the ground as if in prayer.
The yew trees add their sombre pagan thoughts.
The limestone here is fossiliferous
With shells and molluscs from an ancient sea
Embedded in the rock's solidity,
Where men with mowers come to cut and strim
The summer-flowering grasses round the graves.
A wedding leaves a casual scattering
Of dried delphinium petals for confetti.
The living walk down avenues of dead
To cross the road and buy a newspaper
Or milk and groceries from the village shop.

The owls at night regard it as their realm,
A place to hunt warm breathing lives to eat.
A constellation paused above an inn,
The Plough is visible above the Plough:
Stars from a galaxy where we begin
Are dead already in the here and now.
The church looks moribund until you need
Its sacred rituals to be sung or said.
The clouds migrate like maps across the sky
While church bells clang out like a ship's in fog.
On this mown acreage of hallowed ground,
The funerary monuments console
With static crosses and a wooden Christ.

A culvert carries water from the hill
Past the believers and the coffined crew
Whose names postpone their anonymity
And dates define a brief longevity,
As chosen flowers propitiate the dream
Of life eternal and immortal time.

QUIZ NIGHT

Forgotten your memorable information?
Quiz Night reveals how much we might have done.
As last year's team we won the wooden spoon.
What was its name? It doesn't matter now.
What is carpology or the Heptateuch?
Name Long John Silver's Parrot. Quickly.

And what's the collective noun for kangaroos?
Where is the Book of Kells? The smallest state?
What's 1884 in Roman numerals?
From what Olympic sport are beards debarred?
And what's the first name of Inspector Morse?
The commonest element in the earth's crust is ...?

In the interval we eat fish and chips
Feeding diminishing cod stocks and fatty acids
To our deteriorating brains and bodies.
Could F.I.B. have stood for Fish In Batter?
The War Memorial presides ignored
Over the Tudorbethan Parish Hall.

A raffle follows and the winners choose
Jam-making kits and recipe books.
In the following sequence what's the next but one ...?
Perhaps we're practising for those oblivions
Before before again or after after
And not in human time but that of atoms.

SCATTER MY ASHES

(Lines not to be read at my funeral)

It's been a privilege and pleasure,
So thanks for having me on earth.
I never really gave full measure
And had no option on my birth.
It's been a blessing and an honour
Tell the doctor and the priest
But now I'm absent and a goner
All euphemisms are deceased.
Speak these words to the assembly
If any, many, few or some
Friends, acquaintances or family
To this ceremonial come.
What to call it now you've started:
Thanksgiving for a chequered life?
Party for the dear departed
Provided by his widowed wife?

Scatter my ashes here or there,
Say I was handsome, debonair
And rarely crude or crabby,
Scatter my ashes to the air
Scatter my ashes anywhere
But not near Wycombe Abbey.

Say I had talent, style and knowledge,
Love and folly, guile and polish,
Bury my body any old where
But not near Radley College.

Praise my words, extol my nous,
Award the world an alpha plus,
Scatter my desiccated dust
But not near Swanbourne House.

Say how much I loved Earth's crust
Scatter me anywhere if you must
And let surviving son and daughter
Say ash to ash and dust to dust
Somewhere near some stretch of water
But nowhere I'd call foreign.
The River Thames or River Severn
Both will do instead of heaven
Or somewhere by the sea in Devon
Because I spent my childhood there
But not near Dawlish Warren.

Scatter my ashes I don't care
Enjoy your happier memories,
Appreciate the fun, food, fizz
And if I could I'd say goodbye.
Goodbye means God be with you, though,
And who knows if he is?

Loved it mostly, many a minute
Life on planet. Loved you all.
Wish I could still re-begin it,
Now I can't. Well, let that fall
While scattered atoms have a ball.
Now who is me and what am I?
Scatter my ashes. Off I go.

SEZINCOTE

South Devon cattle in a herd
Graze beyond a thistled ditch.
House martins nest high in the eaves;
The stone is amber honeycomb.
A wooden bench in memory of
Frances and Gerald Lamb provides
A meadow view of unmown hay,
The red of poppies and the blue
Of cornflowers where a cabbage white
Flies giddily above the green
To creakings of an ancient yew
Up which the ivy tries to climb.
The sky's a clouded August blue
And like a fragment of the sky
A chalkhill blue hinges its wings
And semaphores a living leaf
Near purple clover, yellow vetch.

And in the garden fountains play.
The crescent of the Orangery
Serves Indian tea in China clay.
Round waterlilies red and white
Reflected skies of Gloucestershire
In elongated lily-ponds
Pay homage to the Taj Mahal,
With yews instead of cypresses.

Money and merchandise designed
This Indianized Arcadia,
An English maharajah's dream
Who made his fortune from the raj
And wanted to impress the shires.
Hindu and Moghul styles combine
The Brahmin bulls with minarets.
The chattris and the chajjahs are
Subsumed into a country house
Whose Anglo-Classical indoors
Is opulent and Regency.

There is a garden to explore.
A temple and a Cotswold stream,
A triple-snakehead fountain in
An arboretum banked with flowers.
A clock chimes from the stable block.
A sundial also marks the time,
As do the shadows of the oaks
From which the house derives its name:
It's mentioned in the Domesday book,
This home of English pedigrees
Restored post-war with Kleinwort care.
John Betjeman adored the place
And so do I today at least.

So do not count the princely cost
In exploitation, servitude,
Of this day-trip to paradise
But see the unities alive
In artefacts and artifice
And seize the spirit of the place
To celebrate as at a shrine
The numinous at Sezincote,
With shantih, shalom, om, Amen,
Or with whatever call to prayer
Has meaning now for being here.

SIGNALS

My father whistled in the pursed-lip style,
Clean-shaven cheeks inflating round the pout,
And woodwind sounds of sorts flowed out in trills
Like notes and tootles on his flageolet.
My mother whistled through her bottom teeth,
A tentative release of jaunty tunes.
I imitated them and practised both
Till I had fluency in either tone.
For finding one another round the house,
They had a signal of a three-note chime
Like dotted symbols therefore and because.
He blew 'Where are you?' she a 'Here I am'
And I could intercept them as a boy
Though neither now has breath for where or why.

60 +

Stocks of energy are lower
Body and the brain are slower
Never was much of a goer
Sixty now.

Tell myself to keep on going.
Where's the end? Well, there's no knowing.
Hours go by and time is flowing
Quickly now.

Got the 60 + concessions
But self-question/answer sessions
Start to sound like true confessions
Far too much.

Drink some bubbly. Tonic. Sherry.
Sing a song and make it merry.
Women are consoling (very)
To the touch.

Spring and trees are full of blossom
But the body's playing possum:
Still got teeth though and I floss them
Late at night.

Bolder now I start to moulder.
Photographs of self look older –
Balding head on sagging shoulder
Heaves in sight.

Nothing happens. Keep on trying,
Try again and without lying
Keep on living death-defying
Till the end.

Russet Glade and Autumn Close
Wish I weren't afraid of those
Geriatric bungalows
Around the bend.

SMALL HOURS

Go back to sleep again.
What you have woken from
Is only a private dream,
An introspective film
Projected by the brain.

Do not become depressed,
Nor mindful of the worst
Reproaches of the past
Which need not be rehearsed.
Think only of the best.

Welcome the sunlit mind.
Let now and future time
Relinquish any claim
To undermine or blame
The chances choice declined.

Go back to sleep again.

St Mary's

The two bereaved, the two bereft,
Both touched the vestments and believed,
Then held each other's hand and wept
For those bereft and those bereaved.

There in the presence of a cross
And of the cross they had to bear
They felt a lessening of their loss
And gained a strength beyond despair.

Each mother who had lost a child
To violence or to sudden death
Had felt in no way reconciled
To grief or its aggrieved distress.

Bereaved, bereft of words to say,
They thought of words as if in prayer
Bowing their heads as if to pray
For help in finding solace there.

Nothing alleviates the pain
For the bereaved or the bereft.
No explanation could explain
In all the hours they had not slept.

What should the children's children know?
What truth about the adult deaths?
Where could the empty questions go
When breath could neither breed nor bless?

And there for minutes as they stood
With harrowed looks on hallowed ground,
Mothers bereft of motherhood
Found something left in what they found.

Unflinchingly and undeceived,
They gained new strength from a despair.
They touched the vestments and believed
In what the living have to share.

STAFFORDSHIRE HOARD

The tiny garnets are set in gold
To glint and glow like blood congealed.

Gold helmet fittings come to grips
With gleaming hilts and pommel caps.

Two golden eagles hold a fish,
Gold talons buried in its flesh.

A crumpled Christ-less golden cross
Reiterates the risen corpse

Leaving strange animals intertwined
In filigrees of mind and mound

Till garnet and glass, cleansed bead by bead,
Fix fire and ice inside a stud.

The golden spirals of its mane
Herald a horse head made for man.

There is inside this war-like cache
No womanly jewel or homely brooch.

Warriors and wearers, what of them
Now nowhere near their treasure's tomb?

Gold under gravel and gone to earth,
Their metals now no mortal myth.

TAMERTON FOLIOT

in memory of Simon Curtis
(1942–2014)

I cycled here as a boy
up to the Dewhursts' farm
where Charlie and Sarah lived
but Memory Lane has changed
with so many houses here
and Simon is wheelchair-bound
with Parkinson's in his hand
and cancerous growths on his spine.
His right hand holds the controls
and family photographs line
the window ledge and walls.

The big man cries like a boy
and I don't know what to say
but I say it anyway,
putting my arm round his back
as if we could still scrum down
in some geriatric pack.
He soon recovers and says:
Well, this is how it is
and this is who I am.
I ask him to read aloud
two poems of his own choice:
one on a Monopoly game
and another about the Home
and collecting sloes with his mother
whom he visited every day.

He's seventy now this year
and a little more deaf than before.
Brown eyes and mind are alert
but body is under the weather
or whatever evasive phrase
can get us through the nights
and diminishing days together.

While he was hoisted up
from wheelchair into his bed,
I walked the perimeter
of Cann House grounds, a walk
he himself recommended
but had never yet been on.
The garden was overgrown
where Victorian servants once
must have gardened and tended.
I looked over the balcony
towards the sound of a stream
talking its way to the Tamar
and saw there looking at me
the delicate face of a deer,
a fallow deer with white tail
which turned and disappeared
into the undergrowth shade.

All our advisors are busy. Please hold
and we will answer your call as quickly as possible.
Your current queue position is 41.
Please be aware that Admissions are only able
to answer enquiries concerning admissions.
If your query relates to another matter
please ring the universal switchboard
via the appropriate number and procedures.
You may also find the answers to your queries
in our user-friendly online enquiry service
and its system for Frequently Unanswered Questions
at www.passageoftime.com forward slash FUQs.

Your current queue position is 53. Please be patient
until it matches your age in calendar years
but may we suggest that while waiting
you enter for the Post Code Lottery,
our current commercial partners in this enterprise?
Should you wish to comment on our services,
either by way of compliment or even complaint,
press the hashtag now, followed by the star key.
All we are made of is really star dust
but have you considered how very remarkable it is
that a disembodied voice can enter your mind
and utter these sounds and signifiers?
If you do not like the intermittent electronic music
and think The Blue Danube followed by
Big Spender and The Hallelujah Chorus
inappropriate to your cultural aspirations,
you may voice or whistle your alternative suggestions
on our interactive forum.

Please be aware that this automated message
can also be heard in over 75 other world languages.
Frequently unanswered questions include or begin with:
Who? What? When? Where? How? And above all why?
Do not let anger get the better of you in the wait for
    fulfilment.
Try not to express frustration in expletives or profanities.
The options open to you are limited by
inter alia money, time, genetics, will-power,
neuroscience and external events.
All our advisors are still busy. Please hold.

The spy was tortured till he told the lie.
The lie was what his captors longed to hear.
They knew there was some hidden reason why
He had not told the whole truth long before.

In simple truth he did not want to die;
They needed a just cause to go to war.
The pain inflicted was too much to bear
And so he told them where the weapons were.

Another terrorist and prisoner
Was bribed with future freedoms to declare
How true the lie was till it soon unloosed
The cause and the occasion of the war.

The minister believed or said he did
The nature of the evidence produced
And from these lies eight million people died,
Militias murdered and civilians fled.

TINEOLA BISSELLIELLA

Everything that lives is holy
but not the larvae of the moth
which leaves all lambswool knitwear holey
and punctuates best woollen cloth.

Most other creatures have my blessing
even rat and sometimes mouse,
but not this beige unprepossessing
moth without a proper mouth.

Its caterpillars do the damage,
microscopic larval beasts,
as in our drawers they munch and ravage
for cashmere wool and mohair feasts.

And when the hatchling moths emerge
from cottons, linen, silk and wool,
they follow what must be their urge
to flap and scuttle on the pull.

They lay their eggs (oviposition)
on dirty fabrics we have shed
and after mating/parturition
both male and female moth lie dead.

So I've erected pheromone traps,
those cardboard tents where they get stuck
whose scent attracts the flapless chaps
who thought it meant a mega-fuck.

TROUT

At first we saw just one,
one brown trout in the stream
using both tail and fin
against the current's strum
to keep its trout brown head
pointing against the weed
which flowered, flowed and swayed
over the riverbed,
under the thistledown
in early evening sun
until we noticed more;
both of us counted them
and made it ten, then twelve,
all pointing up the stream
and keeping their place with skill
so that they seemed themselves
creatures at peace and still
configured in a shoal,
if there are words at all
for a once perfect whole
kept in the mind for a while
to remind it of the soul
and twelve trout in a stream
widening into a pool.

Thinking about tulips and their origins
in eastern Turkey or Armenia,
I wander in the mind and wonder too
what I'm avoiding now by doing so.
High on the mountainous and limestone slopes
near melt-water, the species tulips grow,
their crinkled leaves unfolding from the bulb
layered like an onion but inedible.
Red flowers attract the pollinators there
and then the bees with ultra-violet sight
gather the dust to feed and fertilise
or in the warmth of petals spend the night
so that their muscles can recuperate.

From tulips wild like these, the tulip bred
and via bees in gardens interbred
before mankind the pollinator freed
most colours of the rainbow but not blue.
Tulips of lapis lazuli appear
only on Islam's blue ceramic tiles.
The flower was revered by Ottoman Turks
and Sultan Ahmed III in Istanbul
and thence to Europe and the Netherlands.

So now I feast upon a catalogue,
names, colours, shapes and their imagined scents:
rose apricot and coral with old silk,
Menton Exotic and La Belle Epoque,
Temple of Beauty, Daydream and Dordogne,
The textured feel of petals in the hand
cupped like a glass of wine: Red Emperor.
Pink, orange, purple, yellow, red and white,
Ballade and Ballerina (both sold out).
From Flaming Parrot to Antarctica,
The pallid bulbs in their brown tunic skins
belie the rich exotica to come:
Burgundy Lace or Jazz and Marilyn.
And what, with tens of tulips, are we buying?
Hopes for tomorrow in a death-delaying
blazon of colours for the garden's future,
a promise of perfection for a time
against our own and their eternal dying.

VILLA POOL

How blue the water is
on which the sunlight plays,
filtered by olive trees:
on cross–currents and waves,
specular highlights dance
in glittering, gleaming glints
that water's movement makes
out of fragmented light.

Above the aqua blue,
a yellow butterfly
zigzags across the pool
where underwater too
its shadow briefly swims
and then goes on its way
towards the flowering plants
in search of ... what and why?

A swift descends and skims
the surface of this lake
of human artifice
for insects with struggling limbs
and takes one in full flight
hardly dipping its wings
and then another swift
repeats the moment twice.

Sunbeds and deck-chairs lie
around the oblong pool,
angled to catch the rays
or to enjoy the shade
under the parasol;
a time-switch or some such
releases into the pool
a gentle waterfall.

Ripples and waves subside
to an equilibrium,
until two cypresses,
Italianate in shape,
resolve themselves at night
into reflections of
a graveyard or a grave
and absence of the light.

WALK IN THE RAIN

You can read in the stone
eras of erosion
before you were born
or humans a notion.

And what will it be
when we're dead and gone
but rock against sea,
ocean on stone?

Crags on the shore,
cliffs in the gorge
were formed in the fire
of the mantle's forge.

Continents split,
oceans ice over
and atomized feet
tread nowhere forever.

The paintings grant their fame's fulfilment.
With all that scrambled egg and gilded fruit,
even the frames themselves are works of art.
A Fragonard of fragile boyish beauty
attracts the gaze of visitors until
one sees the nubile female on a swing
with petticoats and footwear flying high,
a connoisseur about to catch the slipper.

And there he is – the son of Rembrandt,
Titus who died in his mid-twenties like
tubercular Richard Parkes Bonington
painting his seascapes and the River Seine
with sky and sea both emptied of himself.
Attendants chat about their annual leave
watched by Infantas and the crucifixion.
The Cavalier's not laughing any more
so much as smiling at the centuries,
each dancing to the music of its time.
The plump pink buttocks of three goddesses
are vexing Paris with a value judgement.
A boy brings fresh-baked bread in a basket
To a matron in an apron at a doorway.

Visitors hold their phones to photograph
illicitly these windows on the silent past.
A husband shows his pregnant wife
the celebration of a birth in Holland.

How different from the staid nativities,
Madonna, child and holy family,
as it's more like a riotous tavern scene
with baby held aloft in red papoose
by a triumphant aging father figure,
though his paternity is called in question.
The household celebrates in raucous style
as mother or child may not last long.
A scatter of broken eggshells streaks the floor.

A baleen whale in search of krill
has dragged a lobster pot for miles.

In a seal pup's neck a gill-net cuts
a deep wound till it suffocates.

A turtle eats the see-through flesh
of polythene bags for jellyfish.

And where the tuskered walrus feed
mussels ingest our microbeads.

Cola and water bottles float
in rafts of plastic which pollute.

Infected with bacteria,
the coral colonies decay.

A seabird feeds its hungry chick
with broken fragments which get stuck.

Abandoned like the fishing net,
a dolphin fights entanglement.

The creek is full of plastic trash
where flies are feeding on floating fish.

Collecting bottles for petty cash,
the fisherman once can only wish.

WILLOW

Of all the trees, the willow is
The last to lose its yellow leaves
And yet among the first to try
Its newborn growth in early spring
When it can glisten gold and green
As trees come back to life again,
But when it rains it seems to cry,
To hang its head and tear its hair
As down the leaves the water seeps
And forms a droplet on each leaf
And, while the rain and wind are there
To wave its arms and shed a tear,
We think of it as him or her
Although in truth it does not care,
But we need company in grief
And that is why we like to hear
The willow is the one that weeps.

To evade the void and annul the non-entity.
To look at the why and find the I in it.
To examine today and discover the infinite.
To colour the anger and flavour the angst.
To hide in the hurt, explore and exploit it.
To meet with defeat undaunted, undoubted.
To re-read the dead and revitalise voices.
To refute the certitudes and certify doubts.
To define inhumane by refining the human.
To dissemble, re-assemble and find treasures in jumble.
To talk to my selves and hear their inner lives.
Sing songs without words and in worlds without ends.
To question assumptions and reassert quests.
To verify versions and vivify visions.
To understand others and utter their otherness,
Creating new creatures and ditto fresh data.
To grasp in new gratitude the grace of the given.
To venerate flora and reverence fauna.
To cultivate cultures and contemplate cults.
To avoid the unwritten illegible horrors.
To transcend the grievance and vindicate hope.
To perceive the perceptible in the perpetual.
To attempt the impossible and effect the perfectible.
To translate the transient into the intricate.
Verbalise verities and eschew the aversion.
To hint at the gist with hymns to the intimate.
To render the reader both finder and keeper.
To be what I can and become what I am.
To fail and to feel an infallible failure.
To improvise symphonies and solemnize silence.
To love and believe in what all must be leaving.
To know now is ever until it is over.

Some of the poems have already appeared as follows:

'Moonlight' and 'Make and Mend' in *Acumen*,
'Signals' on Poems on the Buses in the Guernsey Festival of
    Literature,
'Dozens' in *Magma*,
'60 +', 'Quiz Night' and 'Graffiti' in *The Interpreter's House*,
'A Moment', 'By Air', 'Happy Retirement', 'Home',
    'One Afternoon', 'New Eyes Each Year', 'Small Hours'
    and 'Willow' in *The Spectator*,
'Neverendum' on the English Association website,
'One Afternoon' and 'Sezincote' on www.poetryatlas.com
'Cellar Dweller' on www.wordsforthewild.co.uk